Retailers Mover's Guide Checklist

I would like to dedicate this book to my family, their continual support inspires me to challenge myself and succeed. The idea for this journal stems from my meeting with Johnny and Gloria, owners of a local moving and storage company who constantly share their wisdom and help others.

How to Use this journal

- This journal offers a checklist for the office manager or person receiving daily calls from a potential client. It also acts as a historical tool capturing the pertinent information needed to record and schedule a job request. This journal quickly becomes a great resource for future follow-ups and informational trends that potential clients are actively seeking.

Retail Mover's Guide Checklist

Greet Customer Good Morning, Happy holiday	**Record Customers Name**
Ask for EMAIL	**Current Address**

Is the Move within city?	○ Local Move	○ Out of Town	
Originating Location	○ Business	○ House	○ Apartment
Destination	○ Residence	○ Storage Unit	
Ask how many rooms	○ 2 Bdrm.	○ 3 Bdrm.	○ 4 Bdrm.
Is there an Upstairs?	○ Yes	○ No	
Exterior sheds or Guest House?			
Special types of furniture?	○ Self-adjusting bed	○ fire safe	○ Piano
REMARKS		○ Spinet ○ Baby Grand ○ Upright	
Types of Appliances	○ Refrigerator ○ Washer/Dryer ○ Freezer,		

Does the customer need packing supplies?	○ Yes	○ No	
1.5 Box	Wardrobe		
3.0 Box	Dishpack		
4.5 Box	TV Box	Tape	
Does the customer need additional Insurance?	○ Yes	○ No	

Offer rate

   ○ 2 men and a truck -
   ○ 3 men and a truck -

Approximate date

Requested date requested

NOTES;

Customer's Email to send company's moving guide

Movers Guide Checklist Summary

Customer Name	
Customer Email	
Customer Address	
Phone Number	
Projected Move Date	
Estimated Hours/ Weight	
Special Instructions/ Additional Notes	
Completion Date	
Call Back /Survey Sent	

Retail Mover's Guide Checklist

Greet Customer Good Morning, Happy holiday	**Record Customers Name**
Ask for EMAIL	**Current Address**

Is the Move within city?	○ Local Move	○ Out of Town	
Originating Location	○ Business	○ House	○ Apartment
Destination	○ Residence	○ Storage Unit	
Ask how many rooms	○ 2 Bdrm.	○ 3 Bdrm.	○ 4 Bdrm.
Is there an Upstairs?	○ Yes	○ No	
Exterior sheds or Guest House?			
Special types of furniture?	○ Self-adjusting bed ○ fire safe	○ Piano	
REMARKS		○ Spinet ○ Baby Grand ○ Upright	
Types of Appliances	○ Refrigerator ○ Washer/Dryer ○ Freezer,		

Does the customer need packing supplies?	○ Yes	○ No	
1.5 Box	Wardrobe		
3.0 Box	Dishpack		
4.5 Box	TV Box	Tape	

Does the customer need additional Insurance?	○ Yes	○ No	

Offer rate

   ○ 2 men and a truck -
   ○ 3 men and a truck -

Approximate date

Requested date requested

NOTES;

Customer's Email to send company's moving guide

Movers Guide Checklist Summary

Customer Name Customer Email	
Customer Address Phone Number	
Projected Move Date	
Estimated Hours/ Weight	
Special Instructions/ Additional Notes Completion Date	
Call Back /Survey Sent	

Retail Mover's Guide Checklist

Greet Customer	Record Customers Name
Good Morning, Happy holiday	
Ask for EMAIL	**Current Address**

Is the Move within city?	○ Local Move	○ Out of Town		
Originating Location	○ Business	○ House	○ Apartment	
Destination	○ Residence	○ Storage Unit		
Ask how many rooms	○ 2 Bdrm.	○ 3 Bdrm.	○ 4 Bdrm.	
Is there an Upstairs?	○ Yes	○ No		

Exterior sheds or Guest House?

Special types of furniture?	○ Self-adjusting bed	○ fire safe	○ Piano
REMARKS		○ Spinet ○ Baby Grand ○ Upright	
Types of Appliances	○ Refrigerator ○ Washer/Dryer ○ Freezer,		

Does the customer need packing supplies?		○ Yes	○ No
1.5 Box	Wardrobe		
3.0 Box	Dishpack		
4.5 Box	TV Box	Tape	

Does the customer need additional Insurance?	○ Yes	○ No

Offer rate

   ○ 2 men and a truck -
   ○ 3 men and a truck -

Approximate date

Requested date requested

NOTES;

Customer's Email to send company's moving guide

Movers Guide Checklist Summary

Customer Name	
Customer Email	
Customer Address	
Phone Number	
Projected Move Date	
Estimated Hours/ Weight	
Special Instructions/ Additional Notes	
Completion Date	
Call Back /Survey Sent	

Retail Mover's Guide Checklist

Greet Customer Good Morning, Happy holiday	Record Customers Name
Ask for EMAIL	Current Address

Is the Move within city? ○ Local Move ○ Out of Town	
Originating Location ○ Business ○ House ○ Apartment	
Destination ○ Residence ○ Storage Unit	
Ask how many rooms ○ 2 Bdrm. ○ 3 Bdrm. ○ 4 Bdrm.	
Is there an Upstairs? ○ Yes ○ No	
Exterior sheds or Guest House?	
Special types of furniture? ○ Self-adjusting bed ○ fire safe ○ Piano 　REMARKS 　　　　　　　　　○ Spinet ○ Baby Grand ○ Upright	
Types of Appliances 　　○ Refrigerator ○ Washer/Dryer ○ Freezer,	
Does the customer need packing supplies? ○ Yes ○ No 1.5 Box 　　　　Wardrobe 3.0 Box 　　　　Dishpack 4.5 Box 　　　TV Box 　　Tape	
Does the customer need additional Insurance? ○ Yes ○ No	
Offer rate 　　○ 2 men and a truck - 　　○ 3 men and a truck -	
Approximate date	
Requested date requested	
NOTES;	
Customer's Email to send company's moving guide	

Movers Guide Checklist Summary

Customer Name	
Customer Email	
Customer Address	
Phone Number	
Projected Move Date	
Estimated Hours/ Weight	
Special Instructions/ Additional Notes	
Completion Date	
Call Back /Survey Sent	

Retail Mover's Guide Checklist

Greet Customer	Record Customers Name
Good Morning, Happy holiday	
Ask for EMAIL	**Current Address**

Is the Move within city?	○ Local Move	○ Out of Town		
Originating Location	○ Business	○ House	○ Apartment	
Destination	○ Residence	○ Storage Unit		
Ask how many rooms	○ 2 Bdrm.	○ 3 Bdrm.	○ 4 Bdrm.	
Is there an Upstairs?	○ Yes	○ No		
Exterior sheds or Guest House?				
Special types of furniture?	○ Self-adjusting bed ○ fire safe	○ Piano		
REMARKS		○ Spinet ○ Baby Grand ○ Upright		
Types of Appliances	○ Refrigerator ○ Washer/Dryer ○ Freezer,			

Does the customer need packing supplies?	○ Yes	○ No
1.5 Box Wardrobe		
3.0 Box Dishpack		
4.5 Box TV Box Tape		

Does the customer need additional Insurance?	○ Yes	○ No
Offer rate		
○ 2 men and a truck - ○ 3 men and a truck -		
Approximate date		
Requested date requested		
NOTES;		
Customer's Email to send company's moving guide		

Movers Guide Checklist Summary

Customer Name	
Customer Email	
Customer Address	
Phone Number	
Projected Move Date	
Estimated Hours/ Weight	
Special Instructions/ Additional Notes	
Completion Date	
Call Back /Survey Sent	

Retail Mover's Guide Checklist

Greet Customer	Record Customers Name
Good Morning, Happy holiday	
Ask for EMAIL	**Current Address**

Is the Move within city?	○ Local Move	○ Out of Town			
Originating Location	○ Business	○ House	○ Apartment		
Destination	○ Residence	○ Storage Unit			
Ask how many rooms	○ 2 Bdrm.	○ 3 Bdrm.	○ 4 Bdrm.		
Is there an Upstairs?	○ Yes	○ No			
Exterior sheds or Guest House?					
Special types of furniture?	○ Self-adjusting bed	○ fire safe	○ Piano		
REMARKS			○ Spinet ○ Baby Grand ○ Upright		
Types of Appliances	○ Refrigerator ○ Washer/Dryer ○ Freezer,				
Does the customer need packing supplies?	○ Yes	○ No			
1.5 Box	Wardrobe				
3.0 Box	Dishpack				
4.5 Box	TV Box	Tape			
Does the customer need additional Insurance?	○ Yes	○ No			
Offer rate					
○ 2 men and a truck - ○ 3 men and a truck -					
Approximate date					
Requested date requested					
NOTES;					
Customer's Email to send company's moving guide					

Movers Guide Checklist Summary

Customer Name	
Customer Email	
Customer Address	
Phone Number	
Projected Move Date	
Estimated Hours/ Weight	
Special Instructions/ Additional Notes	
Completion Date	
Call Back /Survey Sent	

Retail Mover's Guide Checklist

Greet Customer	Record Customers Name
Good Morning, Happy holiday	
Ask for EMAIL	Current Address

	Is the Move within city?	○ Local Move	○ Out of Town	
	Originating Location	○ Business	○ House	○ Apartment
	Destination	○ Residence	○ Storage Unit	
	Ask how many rooms	○ 2 Bdrm.	○ 3 Bdrm.	○ 4 Bdrm.
	Is there an Upstairs?	○ Yes	○ No	
	Exterior sheds or Guest House?			
	Special types of furniture?	○ Self-adjusting bed ○ fire safe	○ Piano	
	REMARKS		○ Spinet ○ Baby Grand ○ Upright	
	Types of Appliances	○ Refrigerator ○ Washer/Dryer ○ Freezer,		

Does the customer need packing supplies?	○ Yes	○ No
1.5 Box	Wardrobe	
3.0 Box	Dishpack	
4.5 Box	TV Box Tape	

Does the customer need additional Insurance?	○ Yes	○ No

Offer rate

- ○ 2 men and a truck -
- ○ 3 men and a truck -

Approximate date

Requested date requested

NOTES;

Customer's Email to send company's moving guide

Movers Guide Checklist Summary

Customer Name	
Customer Email	
Customer Address	
Phone Number	
Projected Move Date	
Estimated Hours/ Weight	
Special Instructions/ Additional Notes	
Completion Date	
Call Back /Survey Sent	

Retail Mover's Guide Checklist

Greet Customer Good Morning, Happy holiday	Record Customers Name
Ask for EMAIL	Current Address

Is the Move within city?	○ Local Move ○ Out of Town
Originating Location	○ Business ○ House ○ Apartment
Destination	○ Residence ○ Storage Unit
Ask how many rooms	○ 2 Bdrm. ○ 3 Bdrm. ○ 4 Bdrm.
Is there an Upstairs?	○ Yes ○ No
Exterior sheds or Guest House?	
Special types of furniture? ○ Self-adjusting bed ○ fire safe ○ Piano REMARKS ○ Spinet ○ Baby Grand ○ Upright	
Types of Appliances ○ Refrigerator ○ Washer/Dryer ○ Freezer,	
Does the customer need packing supplies? ○ Yes ○ No 1.5 Box Wardrobe 3.0 Box Dishpack 4.5 Box TV Box Tape	
Does the customer need additional Insurance? ○ Yes ○ No	

Offer rate
 	
     ○ 2 men and a truck -
     ○ 3 men and a truck -	

Approximate date	
Requested date requested	
NOTES;	
Customer's Email to send company's moving guide	

Movers Guide Checklist Summary

Customer Name Customer Email	
Customer Address Phone Number	
Projected Move Date	
Estimated Hours/ Weight	
Special Instructions/ Additional Notes Completion Date	
Call Back /Survey Sent	

Retail Mover's Guide Checklist

Greet Customer	Record Customers Name
Good Morning, Happy holiday	
Ask for EMAIL	**Current Address**

Is the Move within city?	○ Local Move	○ Out of Town	
Originating Location	○ Business	○ House	○ Apartment
Destination	○ Residence	○ Storage Unit	
Ask how many rooms	○ 2 Bdrm.	○ 3 Bdrm.	○ 4 Bdrm.
Is there an Upstairs?	○ Yes	○ No	

Exterior sheds or Guest House?

Special types of furniture?	○ Self-adjusting bed	○ fire safe	○ Piano
REMARKS		○ Spinet ○ Baby Grand ○ Upright	

Types of Appliances   ○ Refrigerator ○ Washer/Dryer ○ Freezer,

Does the customer need packing supplies?	○ Yes	○ No
1.5 Box	Wardrobe	
3.0 Box	Dishpack	
4.5 Box	TV Box Tape	

Does the customer need additional Insurance?	○ Yes	○ No

Offer rate

    ○ 2 men and a truck -
    ○ 3 men and a truck -

Approximate date

Requested date requested

NOTES;

Customer's Email to send company's moving guide

Movers Guide Checklist Summary

Customer Name	
Customer Email	
Customer Address	
Phone Number	
Projected Move Date	
Estimated Hours/ Weight	
Special Instructions/ Additional Notes	
Completion Date	
Call Back /Survey Sent	

Retail Mover's Guide Checklist

Greet Customer Good Morning, Happy holiday	**Record Customers Name**
Ask for EMAIL	**Current Address**

Is the Move within city? ○ Local Move ○ Out of Town
Originating Location ○ Business ○ House ○ Apartment
Destination ○ Residence ○ Storage Unit
Ask how many rooms ○ 2 Bdrm. ○ 3 Bdrm. ○ 4 Bdrm.
Is there an Upstairs? ○ Yes ○ No
Exterior sheds or Guest House?
Special types of furniture? ○ Self-adjusting bed ○ fire safe ○ Piano   REMARKS ○ Spinet ○ Baby Grand ○ Upright
Types of Appliances ○ Refrigerator ○ Washer/Dryer ○ Freezer,
Does the customer need packing supplies? ○ Yes ○ No   1.5 Box   Wardrobe   3.0 Box   Dishpack   4.5 Box   TV Box   Tape
Does the customer need additional Insurance? ○ Yes ○ No
Offer rate   ○ 2 men and a truck -   ○ 3 men and a truck -
Approximate date
Requested date requested
NOTES;
Customer's Email to send company's moving guide

Movers Guide Checklist Summary

Customer Name	
Customer Email	
Customer Address	
Phone Number	
Projected Move Date	
Estimated Hours/ Weight	
Special Instructions/ Additional Notes	
Completion Date	
Call Back /Survey Sent	

Retail Mover's Guide Checklist

Greet Customer	Record Customers Name
Good Morning, Happy holiday	
Ask for EMAIL	Current Address

Is the Move within city?	○ Local Move	○ Out of Town		
Originating Location	○ Business	○ House	○ Apartment	
Destination	○ Residence	○ Storage Unit		
Ask how many rooms	○ 2 Bdrm.	○ 3 Bdrm.	○ 4 Bdrm.	
Is there an Upstairs?	○ Yes	○ No		
Exterior sheds or Guest House?				
Special types of furniture?	○ Self-adjusting bed ○ fire safe	○ Piano		
REMARKS		○ Spinet ○ Baby Grand ○ Upright		
Types of Appliances	○ Refrigerator ○ Washer/Dryer ○ Freezer,			

Does the customer need packing supplies? ○ Yes ○ No
1.5 Box Wardrobe
3.0 Box Dishpack
4.5 Box TV Box Tape

Does the customer need additional Insurance? ○ Yes ○ No
Offer rate
○ 2 men and a truck -
○ 3 men and a truck -
Approximate date
Requested date requested
NOTES;
Customer's Email to send company's moving guide

Movers Guide Checklist Summary

Customer Name	_____
Customer Email	_____
Customer Address	_____
Phone Number	_____
Projected Move Date	_____
Estimated Hours/ Weight	
Special Instructions/ Additional Notes	_____
Completion Date	_____
Call Back /Survey Sent	

Retail Mover's Guide Checklist

Greet Customer Good Morning, Happy holiday	Record Customers Name
Ask for EMAIL	Current Address

Is the Move within city?	○ Local Move	○ Out of Town	
Originating Location	○ Business	○ House	○ Apartment
Destination	○ Residence	○ Storage Unit	
Ask how many rooms	○ 2 Bdrm.	○ 3 Bdrm.	○ 4 Bdrm.
Is there an Upstairs?	○ Yes	○ No	

Exterior sheds or Guest House?

Special types of furniture?	○ Self-adjusting bed	○ fire safe	○ Piano
REMARKS		○ Spinet ○ Baby Grand ○ Upright	
Types of Appliances	○ Refrigerator ○ Washer/Dryer ○ Freezer,		

Does the customer need packing supplies?	○ Yes	○ No

1.5 Box	Wardrobe	
3.0 Box	Dishpack	
4.5 Box	TV Box	Tape

Does the customer need additional Insurance?	○ Yes	○ No

Offer rate

   ○ 2 men and a truck -
   ○ 3 men and a truck -

Approximate date

Requested date requested

NOTES;

Customer's Email to send company's moving guide

Movers Guide Checklist Summary

Customer Name	_____
Customer Email	_____
Customer Address	_____
Phone Number	_____
Projected Move Date	_____
Estimated Hours/ Weight	
Special Instructions/ Additional Notes	_____
Completion Date	_____
Call Back /Survey Sent	

Retail Mover's Guide Checklist

Greet Customer Good Morning, Happy holiday	Record Customers Name
Ask for EMAIL	Current Address

Is the Move within city? ○ Local Move ○ Out of Town
Originating Location ○ Business ○ House ○ Apartment
Destination ○ Residence ○ Storage Unit
Ask how many rooms ○ 2 Bdrm. ○ 3 Bdrm. ○ 4 Bdrm.
Is there an Upstairs? ○ Yes ○ No
Exterior sheds or Guest House?
Special types of furniture? ○ Self-adjusting bed ○ fire safe ○ Piano REMARKS ○ Spinet ○ Baby Grand ○ Upright
Types of Appliances ○ Refrigerator ○ Washer/Dryer ○ Freezer,
Does the customer need packing supplies? ○ Yes ○ No 1.5 Box Wardrobe 3.0 Box Dishpack 4.5 Box TV Box Tape
Does the customer need additional Insurance? ○ Yes ○ No
Offer rate ○ 2 men and a truck - ○ 3 men and a truck -
Approximate date
Requested date requested
NOTES;
Customer's Email to send company's moving guide

Movers Guide Checklist Summary

Customer Name	
Customer Email	
Customer Address	
Phone Number	
Projected Move Date	
Estimated Hours/ Weight	
Special Instructions/ Additional Notes	
Completion Date	
Call Back /Survey Sent	

Retail Mover's Guide Checklist

Greet Customer	Record Customers Name
Good Morning, Happy holiday	
Ask for EMAIL	**Current Address**

Is the Move within city?	○ Local Move	○ Out of Town		
Originating Location	○ Business	○ House	○ Apartment	
Destination	○ Residence	○ Storage Unit		
Ask how many rooms	○ 2 Bdrm.	○ 3 Bdrm.	○ 4 Bdrm.	
Is there an Upstairs?	○ Yes	○ No		
Exterior sheds or Guest House?				
Special types of furniture?	○ Self-adjusting bed	○ fire safe	○ Piano	
REMARKS		○ Spinet ○ Baby Grand ○ Upright		
Types of Appliances	○ Refrigerator ○ Washer/Dryer ○ Freezer,			

Does the customer need packing supplies?	○ Yes	○ No
1.5 Box	Wardrobe	
3.0 Box	Dishpack	
4.5 Box	TV Box Tape	

Does the customer need additional Insurance?	○ Yes	○ No
Offer rate		
○ 2 men and a truck -		
○ 3 men and a truck -		
Approximate date		
Requested date requested		
NOTES;		
Customer's Email to send company's moving guide		

Movers Guide Checklist Summary

Customer Name	
Customer Email	
Customer Address	
Phone Number	
Projected Move Date	
Estimated Hours/ Weight	
Special Instructions/ Additional Notes	
Completion Date	
Call Back /Survey Sent	

Retail Mover's Guide Checklist

Greet Customer Good Morning, Happy holiday	Record Customers Name
Ask for EMAIL	Current Address

	Is the Move within city?	○ Local Move	○ Out of Town		
	Originating Location	○ Business	○ House	○ Apartment	
	Destination	○ Residence	○ Storage Unit		
	Ask how many rooms	○ 2 Bdrm.	○ 3 Bdrm.	○ 4 Bdrm.	
	Is there an Upstairs?	○ Yes	○ No		
	Exterior sheds or Guest House?				
	Special types of furniture?	○ Self-adjusting bed	○ fire safe	○ Piano	
	REMARKS		○ Spinet ○ Baby Grand ○ Upright		
	Types of Appliances	○ Refrigerator ○ Washer/Dryer ○ Freezer,			
	Does the customer need packing supplies?	○ Yes	○ No		
	1.5 Box Wardrobe 3.0 Box Dishpack 4.5 Box TV Box Tape				
	Does the customer need additional Insurance?	○ Yes	○ No		

	Offer rate
	
	   ○ 2 men and a truck -
	   ○ 3 men and a truck -				

	Approximate date				
	Requested date requested				
	NOTES;				
	Customer's Email to send company's moving guide				

Movers Guide Checklist Summary

Customer Name	
Customer Email	
Customer Address	
Phone Number	
Projected Move Date	
Estimated Hours/ Weight	
Special Instructions/ Additional Notes	
Completion Date	
Call Back /Survey Sent	

Retail Mover's Guide Checklist

Greet Customer Good Morning, Happy holiday	**Record Customers Name**
Ask for EMAIL	**Current Address**

Is the Move within city? ○ Local Move ○ Out of Town
Originating Location ○ Business ○ House ○ Apartment
Destination ○ Residence ○ Storage Unit
Ask how many rooms ○ 2 Bdrm. ○ 3 Bdrm. ○ 4 Bdrm.
Is there an Upstairs? ○ Yes ○ No
Exterior sheds or Guest House?
Special types of furniture? ○ Self-adjusting bed ○ fire safe ○ Piano   REMARKS ○ Spinet ○ Baby Grand ○ Upright
Types of Appliances ○ Refrigerator ○ Washer/Dryer ○ Freezer,
Does the customer need packing supplies? ○ Yes ○ No 1.5 Box   Wardrobe 3.0 Box   Dishpack 4.5 Box   TV Box   Tape
Does the customer need additional Insurance? ○ Yes ○ No

Offer rate
 	
  ○ 2 men and a truck -
  ○ 3 men and a truck -

Approximate date
Requested date requested
NOTES;
Customer's Email to send company's moving guide

Movers Guide Checklist Summary

Customer Name	
Customer Email	
Customer Address	
Phone Number	
Projected Move Date	
Estimated Hours/ Weight	
Special Instructions/ Additional Notes	
Completion Date	
Call Back /Survey Sent	

Retail Mover's Guide Checklist

Greet Customer	Record Customers Name
Good Morning, Happy holiday	
Ask for EMAIL	**Current Address**

Is the Move within city?	○ Local Move ○ Out of Town
Originating Location	○ Business ○ House ○ Apartment
Destination	○ Residence ○ Storage Unit
Ask how many rooms	○ 2 Bdrm. ○ 3 Bdrm. ○ 4 Bdrm.
Is there an Upstairs?	○ Yes ○ No
Exterior sheds or Guest House?	
Special types of furniture? ○ Self-adjusting bed ○ fire safe ○ Piano	
REMARKS ○ Spinet ○ Baby Grand ○ Upright	
Types of Appliances ○ Refrigerator ○ Washer/Dryer ○ Freezer,	
Does the customer need packing supplies? ○ Yes ○ No	
1.5 Box Wardrobe	
3.0 Box Dishpack	
4.5 Box TV Box Tape	
Does the customer need additional Insurance? ○ Yes ○ No	
Offer rate	
○ 2 men and a truck - ○ 3 men and a truck -	
Approximate date	
Requested date requested	
NOTES;	
Customer's Email to send company's moving guide	

Movers Guide Checklist Summary

Customer Name Customer Email	
Customer Address Phone Number	
Projected Move Date	
Estimated Hours/ Weight	
Special Instructions/ Additional Notes Completion Date	
Call Back /Survey Sent	

Retail Mover's Guide Checklist

Greet Customer	Record Customers Name
Good Morning, Happy holiday	
Ask for EMAIL	**Current Address**

Is the Move within city? ○ Local Move ○ Out of Town	
Originating Location ○ Business ○ House ○ Apartment	
Destination ○ Residence ○ Storage Unit	
Ask how many rooms ○ 2 Bdrm. ○ 3 Bdrm. ○ 4 Bdrm.	
Is there an Upstairs? ○ Yes ○ No	
Exterior sheds or Guest House?	
Special types of furniture? ○ Self-adjusting bed ○ fire safe ○ Piano	
REMARKS ○ Spinet ○ Baby Grand ○ Upright	
Types of Appliances ○ Refrigerator ○ Washer/Dryer ○ Freezer,	
Does the customer need packing supplies? ○ Yes ○ No	
1.5 Box Wardrobe	
3.0 Box Dishpack	
4.5 Box TV Box Tape	
Does the customer need additional Insurance? ○ Yes ○ No	
Offer rate	
○ 2 men and a truck - ○ 3 men and a truck -	
Approximate date	
Requested date requested	
NOTES;	
Customer's Email to send company's moving guide	

Movers Guide Checklist Summary

Customer Name	
Customer Email	
Customer Address	
Phone Number	
Projected Move Date	
Estimated Hours/ Weight	
Special Instructions/ Additional Notes	
Completion Date	
Call Back /Survey Sent	

Retail Mover's Guide Checklist

Greet Customer Good Morning, Happy holiday	**Record Customers Name**
Ask for EMAIL	**Current Address**

Is the Move within city?	○ Local Move ○ Out of Town
Originating Location	○ Business ○ House ○ Apartment
Destination	○ Residence ○ Storage Unit
Ask how many rooms	○ 2 Bdrm. ○ 3 Bdrm. ○ 4 Bdrm.
Is there an Upstairs?	○ Yes ○ No
Exterior sheds or Guest House?	
Special types of furniture? ○ Self-adjusting bed ○ fire safe ○ Piano REMARKS ○ Spinet ○ Baby Grand ○ Upright	
Types of Appliances ○ Refrigerator ○ Washer/Dryer ○ Freezer,	
Does the customer need packing supplies? ○ Yes ○ No 1.5 Box Wardrobe 3.0 Box Dishpack 4.5 Box TV Box Tape	
Does the customer need additional Insurance? ○ Yes ○ No	

Offer rate
    ○ 2 men and a truck -
    ○ 3 men and a truck -	

Approximate date	
Requested date requested	
NOTES;	
Customer's Email to send company's moving guide	

Movers Guide Checklist Summary

Customer Name	
Customer Email	
Customer Address	
Phone Number	
Projected Move Date	
Estimated Hours/ Weight	
Special Instructions/ Additional Notes	
Completion Date	
Call Back /Survey Sent	

Retail Mover's Guide Checklist

Greet Customer Good Morning, Happy holiday	Record Customers Name
Ask for EMAIL	Current Address

Is the Move within city? ○ Local Move ○ Out of Town	
Originating Location ○ Business ○ House ○ Apartment	
Destination ○ Residence ○ Storage Unit	
Ask how many rooms ○ 2 Bdrm. ○ 3 Bdrm. ○ 4 Bdrm.	
Is there an Upstairs? ○ Yes ○ No	
Exterior sheds or Guest House?	
Special types of furniture? ○ Self-adjusting bed ○ fire safe ○ Piano REMARKS ○ Spinet ○ Baby Grand ○ Upright	
Types of Appliances ○ Refrigerator ○ Washer/Dryer ○ Freezer,	
Does the customer need packing supplies? ○ Yes ○ No 1.5 Box Wardrobe 3.0 Box Dishpack 4.5 Box TV Box Tape	
Does the customer need additional Insurance? ○ Yes ○ No	

Offer rate
 	
     ○ 2 men and a truck -
     ○ 3 men and a truck -	

Approximate date	
Requested date requested	
NOTES;	
Customer's Email to send company's moving guide	

Movers Guide Checklist Summary

Customer Name	
Customer Email	
Customer Address	
Phone Number	
Projected Move Date	
Estimated Hours/ Weight	
Special Instructions/ Additional Notes	
Completion Date	
Call Back /Survey Sent	

Retail Mover's Guide Checklist

Greet Customer	Record Customers Name
Good Morning, Happy holiday	
Ask for EMAIL	**Current Address**

	Is the Move within city?	○ Local Move	○ Out of Town	
	Originating Location	○ Business	○ House	○ Apartment
	Destination	○ Residence	○ Storage Unit	
	Ask how many rooms	○ 2 Bdrm.	○ 3 Bdrm.	○ 4 Bdrm.
	Is there an Upstairs?	○ Yes	○ No	
	Exterior sheds or Guest House?			
	Special types of furniture? ○ Self-adjusting bed ○ fire safe ○ Piano			
	REMARKS ○ Spinet ○ Baby Grand ○ Upright			
	Types of Appliances ○ Refrigerator ○ Washer/Dryer ○ Freezer,			
	Does the customer need packing supplies? ○ Yes ○ No			
	1.5 Box Wardrobe			
	3.0 Box Dishpack			
	4.5 Box TV Box Tape			
	Does the customer need additional Insurance? ○ Yes ○ No			
	Offer rate			
	○ 2 men and a truck - ○ 3 men and a truck -			
	Approximate date			
	Requested date requested			
	NOTES;			
	Customer's Email to send company's moving guide			

Movers Guide Checklist Summary

Customer Name	_____
Customer Email	_____
Customer Address	_____
Phone Number	_____
Projected Move Date	_____
Estimated Hours/ Weight	
Special Instructions/ Additional Notes	_____
Completion Date	_____
Call Back /Survey Sent	

Retail Mover's Guide Checklist

Greet Customer	Record Customers Name
Good Morning, Happy holiday	
Ask for EMAIL	**Current Address**

	Is the Move within city?	○ Local Move	○ Out of Town	
	Originating Location	○ Business	○ House	○ Apartment
	Destination	○ Residence	○ Storage Unit	
	Ask how many rooms	○ 2 Bdrm.	○ 3 Bdrm.	○ 4 Bdrm.
	Is there an Upstairs?	○ Yes	○ No	
	Exterior sheds or Guest House?			
	Special types of furniture?	○ Self-adjusting bed ○ fire safe	○ Piano	
	REMARKS	○ Spinet ○ Baby Grand ○ Upright		
	Types of Appliances	○ Refrigerator ○ Washer/Dryer ○ Freezer,		
	Does the customer need packing supplies?	○ Yes	○ No	
	1.5 Box Wardrobe			
	3.0 Box Dishpack			
	4.5 Box TV Box Tape			
	Does the customer need additional Insurance?	○ Yes	○ No	
	Offer rate			
	○ 2 men and a truck - ○ 3 men and a truck -			
	Approximate date			
	Requested date requested			
	NOTES;			
	Customer's Email to send company's moving guide			

Movers Guide Checklist Summary

Customer Name	
Customer Email	
Customer Address	
Phone Number	
Projected Move Date	
Estimated Hours/ Weight	
Special Instructions/ Additional Notes	
Completion Date	
Call Back /Survey Sent	

Retail Mover's Guide Checklist

Greet Customer Good Morning, Happy holiday	**Record Customers Name**
Ask for EMAIL	**Current Address**

Is the Move within city?	○ Local Move	○ Out of Town	
Originating Location	○ Business	○ House	○ Apartment
Destination	○ Residence	○ Storage Unit	
Ask how many rooms	○ 2 Bdrm.	○ 3 Bdrm.	○ 4 Bdrm.
Is there an Upstairs?	○ Yes	○ No	
Exterior sheds or Guest House?			
Special types of furniture?	○ Self-adjusting bed ○ fire safe	○ Piano	
REMARKS		○ Spinet ○ Baby Grand ○ Upright	
Types of Appliances	○ Refrigerator ○ Washer/Dryer ○ Freezer,		

Does the customer need packing supplies?	○ Yes	○ No	
1.5 Box	Wardrobe		
3.0 Box	Dishpack		
4.5 Box	TV Box	Tape	
Does the customer need additional Insurance?	○ Yes	○ No	
Offer rate			
○ 2 men and a truck - ○ 3 men and a truck -			
Approximate date			
Requested date requested			
NOTES;			
Customer's Email to send company's moving guide			

Movers Guide Checklist Summary

Customer Name Customer Email	
Customer Address Phone Number	
Projected Move Date	
Estimated Hours/ Weight	
Special Instructions/ Additional Notes Completion Date	
Call Back /Survey Sent	

Retail Mover's Guide Checklist

Greet Customer	Record Customers Name
Good Morning, Happy holiday	
Ask for EMAIL	Current Address

Is the Move within city?	○ Local Move	○ Out of Town		
Originating Location	○ Business	○ House	○ Apartment	
Destination	○ Residence	○ Storage Unit		
Ask how many rooms	○ 2 Bdrm.	○ 3 Bdrm.	○ 4 Bdrm.	
Is there an Upstairs?	○ Yes	○ No		
Exterior sheds or Guest House?				
Special types of furniture?	○ Self-adjusting bed ○ fire safe	○ Piano		
REMARKS		○ Spinet ○ Baby Grand ○ Upright		
Types of Appliances	○ Refrigerator ○ Washer/Dryer ○ Freezer,			

Does the customer need packing supplies?	○ Yes	○ No
1.5 Box	Wardrobe	
3.0 Box	Dishpack	
4.5 Box	TV Box Tape	

Does the customer need additional Insurance?	○ Yes	○ No
Offer rate		
○ 2 men and a truck -		
○ 3 men and a truck -		
Approximate date		
Requested date requested		
NOTES;		
Customer's Email to send company's moving guide		

Movers Guide Checklist Summary

Customer Name	
Customer Email	
Customer Address	
Phone Number	
Projected Move Date	
Estimated Hours/ Weight	
Special Instructions/ Additional Notes	
Completion Date	
Call Back /Survey Sent	

Retail Mover's Guide Checklist

Greet Customer Good Morning, Happy holiday	**Record Customers Name**
Ask for EMAIL	**Current Address**

Is the Move within city?	○ Local Move	○ Out of Town	
Originating Location	○ Business	○ House	○ Apartment
Destination	○ Residence	○ Storage Unit	
Ask how many rooms	○ 2 Bdrm.	○ 3 Bdrm.	○ 4 Bdrm.
Is there an Upstairs?	○ Yes	○ No	
Exterior sheds or Guest House?			
Special types of furniture?	○ Self-adjusting bed ○ fire safe	○ Piano	
REMARKS		○ Spinet ○ Baby Grand ○ Upright	
Types of Appliances	○ Refrigerator ○ Washer/Dryer ○ Freezer,		
Does the customer need packing supplies?	○ Yes	○ No	
1.5 Box Wardrobe			
3.0 Box Dishpack			
4.5 Box TV Box Tape			
Does the customer need additional Insurance?	○ Yes	○ No	

Offer rate
 	
    ○ 2 men and a truck -
    ○ 3 men and a truck -			

Approximate date			
Requested date requested			
NOTES;			
Customer's Email to send company's moving guide			

Movers Guide Checklist Summary

Customer Name	
Customer Email	
Customer Address	
Phone Number	
Projected Move Date	
Estimated Hours/ Weight	
Special Instructions/ Additional Notes	
Completion Date	
Call Back /Survey Sent	

Retail Mover's Guide Checklist

Greet Customer Good Morning, Happy holiday	Record Customers Name
Ask for EMAIL	Current Address

Is the Move within city? ○ Local Move ○ Out of Town	
Originating Location ○ Business ○ House ○ Apartment	
Destination ○ Residence ○ Storage Unit	
Ask how many rooms ○ 2 Bdrm. ○ 3 Bdrm. ○ 4 Bdrm.	
Is there an Upstairs? ○ Yes ○ No	
Exterior sheds or Guest House?	
Special types of furniture? ○ Self-adjusting bed ○ fire safe ○ Piano REMARKS ○ Spinet ○ Baby Grand ○ Upright	
Types of Appliances ○ Refrigerator ○ Washer/Dryer ○ Freezer,	
Does the customer need packing supplies? ○ Yes ○ No 1.5 Box Wardrobe 3.0 Box Dishpack 4.5 Box TV Box Tape	
Does the customer need additional Insurance? ○ Yes ○ No	

Offer rate
   ○ 2 men and a truck -
   ○ 3 men and a truck -	

Approximate date	
Requested date requested	
NOTES;	
Customer's Email to send company's moving guide	

Movers Guide Checklist Summary

Customer Name	
Customer Email	
Customer Address	
Phone Number	
Projected Move Date	
Estimated Hours/ Weight	
Special Instructions/ Additional Notes	
Completion Date	
Call Back /Survey Sent	

Retail Mover's Guide Checklist

Greet Customer	Record Customers Name
Good Morning, Happy holiday	
Ask for EMAIL	**Current Address**

Is the Move within city?	○ Local Move	○ Out of Town		
Originating Location	○ Business	○ House	○ Apartment	
Destination	○ Residence	○ Storage Unit		
Ask how many rooms	○ 2 Bdrm.	○ 3 Bdrm.	○ 4 Bdrm.	
Is there an Upstairs?	○ Yes	○ No		
Exterior sheds or Guest House?				
Special types of furniture?	○ Self-adjusting bed	○ fire safe	○ Piano	
REMARKS		○ Spinet ○ Baby Grand ○ Upright		
Types of Appliances	○ Refrigerator ○ Washer/Dryer ○ Freezer,			

Does the customer need packing supplies?	○ Yes	○ No	
1.5 Box	Wardrobe		
3.0 Box	Dishpack		
4.5 Box	TV Box	Tape	
Does the customer need additional Insurance?	○ Yes	○ No	
Offer rate			
○ 2 men and a truck -			
○ 3 men and a truck -			
Approximate date			
Requested date requested			
NOTES;			
Customer's Email to send company's moving guide			

Movers Guide Checklist Summary

Customer Name	
Customer Email	
Customer Address	
Phone Number	
Projected Move Date	
Estimated Hours/ Weight	
Special Instructions/ Additional Notes	
Completion Date	
Call Back /Survey Sent	

Retail Mover's Guide Checklist

Greet Customer	Record Customers Name
Good Morning, Happy holiday	
Ask for EMAIL	**Current Address**

Is the Move within city?	○ Local Move	○ Out of Town	
Originating Location	○ Business	○ House	○ Apartment
Destination	○ Residence	○ Storage Unit	
Ask how many rooms	○ 2 Bdrm.	○ 3 Bdrm.	○ 4 Bdrm.
Is there an Upstairs?	○ Yes	○ No	

Exterior sheds or Guest House?

Special types of furniture?	○ Self-adjusting bed	○ fire safe	○ Piano
REMARKS		○ Spinet ○ Baby Grand ○ Upright	

Types of Appliances ○ Refrigerator ○ Washer/Dryer ○ Freezer,

Does the customer need packing supplies?   ○ Yes   ○ No

1.5 Box	Wardrobe
3.0 Box	Dishpack
4.5 Box	TV Box Tape

Does the customer need additional Insurance?   ○ Yes   ○ No

Offer rate

○ 2 men and a truck -
○ 3 men and a truck -

Approximate date

Requested date requested

NOTES;

Customer's Email to send company's moving guide

Movers Guide Checklist Summary

Customer Name	
Customer Email	
Customer Address	
Phone Number	
Projected Move Date	
Estimated Hours/ Weight	
Special Instructions/ Additional Notes	
Completion Date	
Call Back /Survey Sent	

Retail Mover's Guide Checklist

Greet Customer Good Morning, Happy holiday	**Record Customers Name**
Ask for EMAIL	**Current Address**

Is the Move within city?	○ Local Move	○ Out of Town	
Originating Location	○ Business	○ House	○ Apartment
Destination	○ Residence	○ Storage Unit	
Ask how many rooms	○ 2 Bdrm.	○ 3 Bdrm.	○ 4 Bdrm.
Is there an Upstairs?	○ Yes	○ No	

Exterior sheds or Guest House?

Special types of furniture?	○ Self-adjusting bed	○ fire safe	○ Piano
REMARKS		○ Spinet ○ Baby Grand ○ Upright	

Types of Appliances   ○ Refrigerator ○ Washer/Dryer ○ Freezer,

Does the customer need packing supplies?	○ Yes	○ No
1.5 Box	Wardrobe	
3.0 Box	Dishpack	
4.5 Box	TV Box	Tape

Does the customer need additional Insurance?	○ Yes	○ No

Offer rate

    ○ 2 men and a truck -
    ○ 3 men and a truck -

Approximate date

Requested date requested

NOTES;

Customer's Email to send company's moving guide

Movers Guide Checklist Summary

Customer Name	
Customer Email	
Customer Address	
Phone Number	
Projected Move Date	
Estimated Hours/ Weight	
Special Instructions/ Additional Notes	
Completion Date	
Call Back /Survey Sent	

Retail Mover's Guide Checklist

Greet Customer	Record Customers Name
Good Morning, Happy holiday	
Ask for EMAIL	**Current Address**

	Is the Move within city?	○ Local Move	○ Out of Town	
	Originating Location	○ Business	○ House	○ Apartment
	Destination	○ Residence	○ Storage Unit	
	Ask how many rooms	○ 2 Bdrm.	○ 3 Bdrm.	○ 4 Bdrm.
	Is there an Upstairs?	○ Yes	○ No	
	Exterior sheds or Guest House?			
	Special types of furniture? ○ Self-adjusting bed ○ fire safe ○ Piano			
	REMARKS ○ Spinet ○ Baby Grand ○ Upright			
	Types of Appliances ○ Refrigerator ○ Washer/Dryer ○ Freezer,			
	Does the customer need packing supplies? ○ Yes ○ No			
	1.5 Box Wardrobe			
	3.0 Box Dishpack			
	4.5 Box TV Box Tape			
	Does the customer need additional Insurance? ○ Yes ○ No			
	Offer rate			
	○ 2 men and a truck - ○ 3 men and a truck -			
	Approximate date			
	Requested date requested			
	NOTES;			
	Customer's Email to send company's moving guide			

Movers Guide Checklist Summary

Customer Name	_____
Customer Email	_____
Customer Address	_____
Phone Number	_____
Projected Move Date	_____
Estimated Hours/ Weight	
Special Instructions/ Additional Notes	_____
Completion Date	_____
Call Back /Survey Sent	

Retail Mover's Guide Checklist

Greet Customer	Record Customers Name
Good Morning, Happy holiday	
Ask for EMAIL	**Current Address**

Is the Move within city?	○ Local Move	○ Out of Town		
Originating Location	○ Business	○ House	○ Apartment	
Destination	○ Residence	○ Storage Unit		
Ask how many rooms	○ 2 Bdrm.	○ 3 Bdrm.	○ 4 Bdrm.	
Is there an Upstairs?	○ Yes	○ No		
Exterior sheds or Guest House?				
Special types of furniture?	○ Self-adjusting bed	○ fire safe	○ Piano	
REMARKS		○ Spinet ○ Baby Grand ○ Upright		
Types of Appliances	○ Refrigerator ○ Washer/Dryer ○ Freezer,			

Does the customer need packing supplies?	○ Yes	○ No
1.5 Box	Wardrobe	
3.0 Box	Dishpack	
4.5 Box	TV Box	Tape

Does the customer need additional Insurance?	○ Yes	○ No

Offer rate	
○ 2 men and a truck -	
○ 3 men and a truck -	

Approximate date
Requested date requested
NOTES;
Customer's Email to send company's moving guide

Movers Guide Checklist Summary

Customer Name	
Customer Email	
Customer Address	
Phone Number	
Projected Move Date	
Estimated Hours/ Weight	
Special Instructions/ Additional Notes	
Completion Date	
Call Back /Survey Sent	

Retail Mover's Guide Checklist

Greet Customer Good Morning, Happy holiday	**Record Customers Name**
Ask for EMAIL	**Current Address**

Is the Move within city?	○ Local Move	○ Out of Town		
Originating Location	○ Business	○ House	○ Apartment	
Destination	○ Residence	○ Storage Unit		
Ask how many rooms	○ 2 Bdrm.	○ 3 Bdrm.	○ 4 Bdrm.	
Is there an Upstairs?	○ Yes	○ No		
Exterior sheds or Guest House?				
Special types of furniture?	○ Self-adjusting bed	○ fire safe	○ Piano	
REMARKS		○ Spinet ○ Baby Grand ○ Upright		
Types of Appliances	○ Refrigerator ○ Washer/Dryer ○ Freezer,			

Does the customer need packing supplies?	○ Yes	○ No	
1.5 Box	Wardrobe		
3.0 Box	Dishpack		
4.5 Box	TV Box	Tape	
Does the customer need additional Insurance?	○ Yes	○ No	
Offer rate			
○ 2 men and a truck - ○ 3 men and a truck -			
Approximate date			
Requested date requested			
NOTES;			
Customer's Email to send company's moving guide			

Movers Guide Checklist Summary

Customer Name	
Customer Email	
Customer Address	
Phone Number	
Projected Move Date	
Estimated Hours/ Weight	
Special Instructions/ Additional Notes	
Completion Date	
Call Back /Survey Sent	

Retail Mover's Guide Checklist

Greet Customer Good Morning, Happy holiday	**Record Customers Name**
Ask for EMAIL	**Current Address**

Is the Move within city?	○ Local Move	○ Out of Town		
Originating Location	○ Business	○ House	○ Apartment	
Destination	○ Residence	○ Storage Unit		
Ask how many rooms	○ 2 Bdrm.	○ 3 Bdrm.	○ 4 Bdrm.	
Is there an Upstairs?	○ Yes	○ No		
Exterior sheds or Guest House?				
Special types of furniture?	○ Self-adjusting bed	○ fire safe	○ Piano	
REMARKS			○ Spinet ○ Baby Grand ○ Upright	
Types of Appliances	○ Refrigerator ○ Washer/Dryer ○ Freezer,			

Does the customer need packing supplies?		○ Yes	○ No
1.5 Box	Wardrobe		
3.0 Box	Dishpack		
4.5 Box	TV Box	Tape	
Does the customer need additional Insurance?		○ Yes	○ No

Offer rate
 	
  ○ 2 men and a truck -
  ○ 3 men and a truck -			

Approximate date			
Requested date requested			
NOTES;			
Customer's Email to send company's moving guide			

Movers Guide Checklist Summary

Customer Name	_____
Customer Email	_____
Customer Address	_____
Phone Number	_____
Projected Move Date	_____
Estimated Hours/ Weight	
Special Instructions/ Additional Notes	_____
Completion Date	_____
Call Back /Survey Sent	

Retail Mover's Guide Checklist

Greet Customer Good Morning, Happy holiday	Record Customers Name
Ask for EMAIL	Current Address

Is the Move within city? ○ Local Move ○ Out of Town	
Originating Location ○ Business ○ House ○ Apartment	
Destination ○ Residence ○ Storage Unit	
Ask how many rooms ○ 2 Bdrm. ○ 3 Bdrm. ○ 4 Bdrm.	
Is there an Upstairs? ○ Yes ○ No	
Exterior sheds or Guest House?	
Special types of furniture? ○ Self-adjusting bed ○ fire safe ○ Piano REMARKS ○ Spinet ○ Baby Grand ○ Upright	
Types of Appliances ○ Refrigerator ○ Washer/Dryer ○ Freezer,	
Does the customer need packing supplies? ○ Yes ○ No 1.5 Box Wardrobe 3.0 Box Dishpack 4.5 Box TV Box Tape	
Does the customer need additional Insurance? ○ Yes ○ No	
Offer rate ○ 2 men and a truck - ○ 3 men and a truck -	
Approximate date	
Requested date requested	
NOTES;	
Customer's Email to send company's moving guide	

Movers Guide Checklist Summary

Customer Name	_____
Customer Email	_____
Customer Address	_____
Phone Number	_____
Projected Move Date	_____
Estimated Hours/ Weight	
Special Instructions/ Additional Notes	_____
Completion Date	_____
Call Back /Survey Sent	

Retail Mover's Guide Checklist

Greet Customer Good Morning, Happy holiday	**Record Customers Name**
Ask for EMAIL	**Current Address**

Is the Move within city?	○ Local Move	○ Out of Town	
Originating Location	○ Business	○ House	○ Apartment
Destination	○ Residence	○ Storage Unit	
Ask how many rooms	○ 2 Bdrm.	○ 3 Bdrm.	○ 4 Bdrm.
Is there an Upstairs?	○ Yes	○ No	
Exterior sheds or Guest House?			
Special types of furniture?	○ Self-adjusting bed ○ fire safe	○ Piano	
REMARKS		○ Spinet ○ Baby Grand ○ Upright	
Types of Appliances	○ Refrigerator ○ Washer/Dryer ○ Freezer,		

Does the customer need packing supplies?	○ Yes	○ No
1.5 Box	Wardrobe	
3.0 Box	Dishpack	
4.5 Box	TV Box	Tape
Does the customer need additional Insurance?	○ Yes	○ No

Offer rate
 	
    ○ 2 men and a truck -
    ○ 3 men and a truck -		

Approximate date		
Requested date requested		
NOTES;		
Customer's Email to send company's moving guide		

Movers Guide Checklist Summary

Customer Name	
Customer Email	
Customer Address	
Phone Number	
Projected Move Date	
Estimated Hours/ Weight	
Special Instructions/ Additional Notes	
Completion Date	
Call Back /Survey Sent	

Retail Mover's Guide Checklist

Greet Customer Good Morning, Happy holiday	**Record Customers Name**
Ask for EMAIL	**Current Address**

Is the Move within city?	○ Local Move	○ Out of Town		
Originating Location	○ Business	○ House	○ Apartment	
Destination	○ Residence	○ Storage Unit		
Ask how many rooms	○ 2 Bdrm.	○ 3 Bdrm.	○ 4 Bdrm.	
Is there an Upstairs?	○ Yes	○ No		
Exterior sheds or Guest House?				
Special types of furniture?	○ Self-adjusting bed	○ fire safe	○ Piano	
REMARKS		○ Spinet ○ Baby Grand ○ Upright		
Types of Appliances	○ Refrigerator ○ Washer/Dryer ○ Freezer,			

Does the customer need packing supplies?	○ Yes	○ No
1.5 Box Wardrobe		
3.0 Box Dishpack		
4.5 Box TV Box Tape		
Does the customer need additional Insurance?	○ Yes	○ No

Offer rate
 	
    ○ 2 men and a truck -
    ○ 3 men and a truck -		

Approximate date		
Requested date requested		
NOTES;		
Customer's Email to send company's moving guide		

Movers Guide Checklist Summary

Customer Name	
Customer Email	
Customer Address	
Phone Number	
Projected Move Date	
Estimated Hours/ Weight	
Special Instructions/ Additional Notes	
Completion Date	
Call Back /Survey Sent	

Retail Mover's Guide Checklist

Greet Customer Good Morning, Happy holiday	Record Customers Name
Ask for EMAIL	Current Address

Is the Move within city? ○ Local Move ○ Out of Town	
Originating Location ○ Business ○ House ○ Apartment	
Destination ○ Residence ○ Storage Unit	
Ask how many rooms ○ 2 Bdrm. ○ 3 Bdrm. ○ 4 Bdrm.	
Is there an Upstairs? ○ Yes ○ No	
Exterior sheds or Guest House?	
Special types of furniture? ○ Self-adjusting bed ○ fire safe ○ Piano REMARKS ○ Spinet ○ Baby Grand ○ Upright	
Types of Appliances ○ Refrigerator○ Washer/Dryer ○ Freezer,	
Does the customer need packing supplies? ○ Yes ○ No 1.5 Box Wardrobe 3.0 Box Dishpack 4.5 Box TV Box Tape	
Does the customer need additional Insurance? ○ Yes ○ No	

Offer rate
 	
     ○ 2 men and a truck -
     ○ 3 men and a truck -	

Approximate date	
Requested date requested	
NOTES;	
Customer's Email to send company's moving guide	

Movers Guide Checklist Summary

Customer Name	
Customer Email	
Customer Address	
Phone Number	
Projected Move Date	
Estimated Hours/ Weight	
Special Instructions/ Additional Notes	
Completion Date	
Call Back /Survey Sent	

Retail Mover's Guide Checklist

Greet Customer Good Morning, Happy holiday	**Record Customers Name**
Ask for EMAIL	**Current Address**

Is the Move within city?	○ Local Move	○ Out of Town	
Originating Location	○ Business	○ House	○ Apartment
Destination	○ Residence	○ Storage Unit	
Ask how many rooms	○ 2 Bdrm.	○ 3 Bdrm.	○ 4 Bdrm.
Is there an Upstairs?	○ Yes	○ No	

Exterior sheds or Guest House?

Special types of furniture?	○ Self-adjusting bed ○ fire safe	○ Piano	
REMARKS		○ Spinet ○ Baby Grand ○ Upright	
Types of Appliances	○ Refrigerator ○ Washer/Dryer ○ Freezer,		

Does the customer need packing supplies?	○ Yes	○ No
1.5 Box Wardrobe		
3.0 Box Dishpack		
4.5 Box TV Box Tape		

Does the customer need additional Insurance?	○ Yes	○ No

Offer rate

   ○ 2 men and a truck -
   ○ 3 men and a truck -

Approximate date

Requested date requested

NOTES;

Customer's Email to send company's moving guide

Movers Guide Checklist Summary

Customer Name	
Customer Email	
Customer Address	
Phone Number	
Projected Move Date	
Estimated Hours/ Weight	
Special Instructions/ Additional Notes	
Completion Date	
Call Back /Survey Sent	

Retail Mover's Guide Checklist

Greet Customer Good Morning, Happy holiday	Record Customers Name
Ask for EMAIL	Current Address

	Is the Move within city?	○ Local Move	○ Out of Town	
	Originating Location	○ Business	○ House	○ Apartment
	Destination	○ Residence	○ Storage Unit	
	Ask how many rooms	○ 2 Bdrm.	○ 3 Bdrm.	○ 4 Bdrm.
	Is there an Upstairs?	○ Yes	○ No	
	Exterior sheds or Guest House?			
	Special types of furniture? ○ Self-adjusting bed ○ fire safe ○ Piano REMARKS ○ Spinet ○ Baby Grand ○ Upright			
	Types of Appliances ○ Refrigerator ○ Washer/Dryer ○ Freezer,			
	Does the customer need packing supplies? ○ Yes ○ No 1.5 Box Wardrobe 3.0 Box Dishpack 4.5 Box TV Box Tape			
	Does the customer need additional Insurance? ○ Yes ○ No			

	Offer rate
	
	  ○ 2 men and a truck -
	  ○ 3 men and a truck -			

	Approximate date			
	Requested date requested			
	NOTES;			
	Customer's Email to send company's moving guide			

Movers Guide Checklist Summary

Customer Name	
Customer Email	
Customer Address	
Phone Number	
Projected Move Date	
Estimated Hours/ Weight	
Special Instructions/ Additional Notes	
Completion Date	
Call Back /Survey Sent	

Retail Mover's Guide Checklist

Greet Customer Good Morning, Happy holiday	Record Customers Name
Ask for EMAIL	Current Address

Is the Move within city?	○ Local Move ○ Out of Town	
Originating Location	○ Business ○ House ○ Apartment	
Destination	○ Residence ○ Storage Unit	
Ask how many rooms	○ 2 Bdrm. ○ 3 Bdrm. ○ 4 Bdrm.	
Is there an Upstairs?	○ Yes ○ No	
Exterior sheds or Guest House?		
Special types of furniture? ○ Self-adjusting bed ○ fire safe ○ Piano REMARKS ○ Spinet ○ Baby Grand ○ Upright		
Types of Appliances ○ Refrigerator ○ Washer/Dryer ○ Freezer,		
Does the customer need packing supplies? ○ Yes ○ No 1.5 Box Wardrobe 3.0 Box Dishpack 4.5 Box TV Box Tape		
Does the customer need additional Insurance? ○ Yes ○ No		

Offer rate
 	
        ○ 2 men and a truck -
        ○ 3 men and a truck -		

Approximate date		
Requested date requested		
NOTES;		
Customer's Email to send company's moving guide		

Movers Guide Checklist Summary

Customer Name	
Customer Email	
Customer Address	
Phone Number	
Projected Move Date	
Estimated Hours/ Weight	
Special Instructions/ Additional Notes	
Completion Date	
Call Back /Survey Sent	

Retail Mover's Guide Checklist

Greet Customer Good Morning, Happy holiday	Record Customers Name
Ask for EMAIL	Current Address

	Is the Move within city?	○ Local Move	○ Out of Town	
	Originating Location	○ Business	○ House	○ Apartment
	Destination	○ Residence	○ Storage Unit	
	Ask how many rooms	○ 2 Bdrm.	○ 3 Bdrm.	○ 4 Bdrm.
	Is there an Upstairs?	○ Yes	○ No	
	Exterior sheds or Guest House?			
	Special types of furniture?	○ Self-adjusting bed ○ fire safe	○ Piano	
	REMARKS		○ Spinet ○ Baby Grand ○ Upright	
	Types of Appliances	○ Refrigerator ○ Washer/Dryer ○ Freezer,		
	Does the customer need packing supplies?	○ Yes	○ No	
	1.5 Box Wardrobe			
	3.0 Box Dishpack			
	4.5 Box TV Box Tape			
	Does the customer need additional Insurance?	○ Yes	○ No	
	Offer rate ○ 2 men and a truck - ○ 3 men and a truck -			
	Approximate date			
	Requested date requested			
	NOTES;			
	Customer's Email to send company's moving guide			

Movers Guide Checklist Summary

Customer Name	_____
Customer Email	_____
Customer Address	_____
Phone Number	_____
Projected Move Date	_____
Estimated Hours/ Weight	
Special Instructions/ Additional Notes	_____
Completion Date	_____
Call Back /Survey Sent	

Retail Mover's Guide Checklist

Greet Customer Good Morning, Happy holiday	**Record Customers Name**
Ask for EMAIL	**Current Address**

Is the Move within city?	○ Local Move ○ Out of Town
Originating Location	○ Business ○ House ○ Apartment
Destination	○ Residence ○ Storage Unit
Ask how many rooms	○ 2 Bdrm. ○ 3 Bdrm. ○ 4 Bdrm.
Is there an Upstairs?	○ Yes ○ No
Exterior sheds or Guest House?	
Special types of furniture? ○ Self-adjusting bed ○ fire safe ○ Piano REMARKS ○ Spinet ○ Baby Grand ○ Upright	
Types of Appliances ○ Refrigerator ○ Washer/Dryer ○ Freezer,	
Does the customer need packing supplies? ○ Yes ○ No 1.5 Box Wardrobe 3.0 Box Dishpack 4.5 Box TV Box Tape	
Does the customer need additional Insurance? ○ Yes ○ No	

Offer rate
 	
  ○ 2 men and a truck -
  ○ 3 men and a truck -	

Approximate date	
Requested date requested	
NOTES;	
Customer's Email to send company's moving guide	

Movers Guide Checklist Summary

Customer Name	_____
Customer Email	_____
Customer Address	_____
Phone Number	_____
Projected Move Date	_____
Estimated Hours/ Weight	
Special Instructions/ Additional Notes	_____
Completion Date	_____
Call Back /Survey Sent	

Retail Mover's Guide Checklist

Greet Customer Good Morning, Happy holiday	Record Customers Name
Ask for EMAIL	Current Address

Is the Move within city?	○ Local Move ○ Out of Town
Originating Location	○ Business ○ House ○ Apartment
Destination	○ Residence ○ Storage Unit
Ask how many rooms	○ 2 Bdrm. ○ 3 Bdrm. ○ 4 Bdrm.
Is there an Upstairs?	○ Yes ○ No
Exterior sheds or Guest House?	
Special types of furniture? ○ Self-adjusting bed ○ fire safe ○ Piano REMARKS ○ Spinet ○ Baby Grand ○ Upright	
Types of Appliances ○ Refrigerator ○ Washer/Dryer ○ Freezer,	
Does the customer need packing supplies? ○ Yes ○ No 1.5 Box Wardrobe 3.0 Box Dishpack 4.5 Box TV Box Tape	
Does the customer need additional Insurance? ○ Yes ○ No	

Offer rate
 	
     ○ 2 men and a truck -
     ○ 3 men and a truck -	

Approximate date	
Requested date requested	
NOTES;	
Customer's Email to send company's moving guide	

Movers Guide Checklist Summary

Customer Name	
Customer Email	
Customer Address	
Phone Number	
Projected Move Date	
Estimated Hours/ Weight	
Special Instructions/ Additional Notes	
Completion Date	
Call Back /Survey Sent	

Retail Mover's Guide Checklist

Greet Customer Good Morning, Happy holiday	Record Customers Name
Ask for EMAIL	Current Address

	Is the Move within city?	○ Local Move	○ Out of Town	
	Originating Location	○ Business	○ House	○ Apartment
	Destination	○ Residence	○ Storage Unit	
	Ask how many rooms	○ 2 Bdrm.	○ 3 Bdrm.	○ 4 Bdrm.
	Is there an Upstairs?	○ Yes	○ No	
	Exterior sheds or Guest House?			
	Special types of furniture? ○ Self-adjusting bed ○ fire safe ○ Piano REMARKS ○ Spinet ○ Baby Grand ○ Upright			
	Types of Appliances ○ Refrigerator ○ Washer/Dryer ○ Freezer,			
	Does the customer need packing supplies? ○ Yes ○ No 1.5 Box Wardrobe 3.0 Box Dishpack 4.5 Box TV Box Tape			
	Does the customer need additional Insurance? ○ Yes ○ No			

	Offer rate
	
	    ○ 2 men and a truck -
	    ○ 3 men and a truck -			

	Approximate date			
	Requested date requested			
	NOTES;			
	Customer's Email to send company's moving guide			

Movers Guide Checklist Summary

Customer Name	
Customer Email	
Customer Address	
Phone Number	
Projected Move Date	
Estimated Hours/ Weight	
Special Instructions/ Additional Notes	
Completion Date	
Call Back /Survey Sent	

Retail Mover's Guide Checklist

Greet Customer Good Morning, Happy holiday	Record Customers Name
Ask for EMAIL	Current Address

Is the Move within city?	○ Local Move ○ Out of Town
Originating Location	○ Business ○ House ○ Apartment
Destination	○ Residence ○ Storage Unit
Ask how many rooms	○ 2 Bdrm. ○ 3 Bdrm. ○ 4 Bdrm.
Is there an Upstairs?	○ Yes ○ No
Exterior sheds or Guest House?	
Special types of furniture?	○ Self-adjusting bed ○ fire safe ○ Piano
REMARKS	○ Spinet ○ Baby Grand ○ Upright
Types of Appliances	○ Refrigerator ○ Washer/Dryer ○ Freezer,
Does the customer need packing supplies?	○ Yes ○ No
1.5 Box Wardrobe 3.0 Box Dishpack 4.5 Box TV Box Tape	
Does the customer need additional Insurance?	○ Yes ○ No

Offer rate
 	
   ○ 2 men and a truck -
   ○ 3 men and a truck -	

Approximate date	
Requested date requested	
NOTES;	
Customer's Email to send company's moving guide	

Movers Guide Checklist Summary

Customer Name	
Customer Email	
Customer Address	
Phone Number	
Projected Move Date	
Estimated Hours/ Weight	
Special Instructions/ Additional Notes	
Completion Date	
Call Back /Survey Sent	

Retail Mover's Guide Checklist

Greet Customer	Record Customers Name
Good Morning, Happy holiday	
Ask for EMAIL	**Current Address**

Is the Move within city?	○ Local Move	○ Out of Town		
Originating Location	○ Business	○ House	○ Apartment	
Destination	○ Residence	○ Storage Unit		
Ask how many rooms	○ 2 Bdrm.	○ 3 Bdrm.	○ 4 Bdrm.	
Is there an Upstairs?	○ Yes	○ No		
Exterior sheds or Guest House?				
Special types of furniture?	○ Self-adjusting bed ○ fire safe	○ Piano		
REMARKS		○ Spinet ○ Baby Grand ○ Upright		
Types of Appliances	○ Refrigerator ○ Washer/Dryer ○ Freezer,			

Does the customer need packing supplies?	○ Yes	○ No
1.5 Box Wardrobe		
3.0 Box Dishpack		
4.5 Box TV Box Tape		
Does the customer need additional Insurance?	○ Yes	○ No
Offer rate		
○ 2 men and a truck - ○ 3 men and a truck -		
Approximate date		
Requested date requested		
NOTES;		
Customer's Email to send company's moving guide		

Movers Guide Checklist Summary

Customer Name	
Customer Email	
Customer Address	
Phone Number	
Projected Move Date	
Estimated Hours/ Weight	
Special Instructions/ Additional Notes	
Completion Date	
Call Back /Survey Sent	

Retail Mover's Guide Checklist

Greet Customer	Record Customers Name
Good Morning, Happy holiday	
Ask for EMAIL	**Current Address**

	Is the Move within city?	○ Local Move	○ Out of Town		
	Originating Location	○ Business	○ House	○ Apartment	
	Destination	○ Residence	○ Storage Unit		
	Ask how many rooms	○ 2 Bdrm.	○ 3 Bdrm.	○ 4 Bdrm.	
	Is there an Upstairs?	○ Yes	○ No		
	Exterior sheds or Guest House?				
	Special types of furniture?	○ Self-adjusting bed ○ fire safe	○ Piano		
	REMARKS		○ Spinet ○ Baby Grand ○ Upright		
	Types of Appliances	○ Refrigerator ○ Washer/Dryer ○ Freezer,			
	Does the customer need packing supplies?	○ Yes	○ No		
	1.5 Box	Wardrobe			
	3.0 Box	Dishpack			
	4.5 Box	TV Box	Tape		
	Does the customer need additional Insurance?	○ Yes	○ No		
	Offer rate				
	○ 2 men and a truck - ○ 3 men and a truck -				
	Approximate date				
	Requested date requested				
	NOTES;				
	Customer's Email to send company's moving guide				

Movers Guide Checklist Summary

Customer Name	_____
Customer Email	_____
Customer Address	_____
Phone Number	_____
Projected Move Date	_____
Estimated Hours/ Weight	
Special Instructions/ Additional Notes	_____
Completion Date	_____
Call Back /Survey Sent	

Retail Mover's Guide Checklist

Greet Customer	Record Customers Name
Good Morning, Happy holiday	
Ask for EMAIL	**Current Address**

	Is the Move within city?	○ Local Move	○ Out of Town	
	Originating Location	○ Business	○ House	○ Apartment
	Destination	○ Residence	○ Storage Unit	
	Ask how many rooms	○ 2 Bdrm.	○ 3 Bdrm.	○ 4 Bdrm.
	Is there an Upstairs?	○ Yes	○ No	
	Exterior sheds or Guest House?			
	Special types of furniture? ○ Self-adjusting bed ○ fire safe ○ Piano			
	REMARKS ○ Spinet ○ Baby Grand ○ Upright			
	Types of Appliances ○ Refrigerator ○ Washer/Dryer ○ Freezer,			
	Does the customer need packing supplies? ○ Yes ○ No			
	1.5 Box Wardrobe			
	3.0 Box Dishpack			
	4.5 Box TV Box Tape			
	Does the customer need additional Insurance? ○ Yes ○ No			
	Offer rate			
	○ 2 men and a truck - ○ 3 men and a truck -			
	Approximate date			
	Requested date requested			
	NOTES;			
	Customer's Email to send company's moving guide			

Movers Guide Checklist Summary

Customer Name	
Customer Email	
Customer Address	
Phone Number	
Projected Move Date	
Estimated Hours/ Weight	
Special Instructions/ Additional Notes	
Completion Date	
Call Back /Survey Sent	

Retail Mover's Guide Checklist

Greet Customer Good Morning, Happy holiday	Record Customers Name
Ask for EMAIL	Current Address

Is the Move within city?	○ Local Move	○ Out of Town		
Originating Location	○ Business	○ House	○ Apartment	
Destination	○ Residence	○ Storage Unit		
Ask how many rooms	○ 2 Bdrm.	○ 3 Bdrm.	○ 4 Bdrm.	
Is there an Upstairs?	○ Yes	○ No		
Exterior sheds or Guest House?				
Special types of furniture?	○ Self-adjusting bed	○ fire safe	○ Piano	
REMARKS		○ Spinet ○ Baby Grand ○ Upright		
Types of Appliances	○ Refrigerator ○ Washer/Dryer ○ Freezer,			

Does the customer need packing supplies?	○ Yes	○ No	
1.5 Box	Wardrobe		
3.0 Box	Dishpack		
4.5 Box	TV Box	Tape	
Does the customer need additional Insurance?	○ Yes	○ No	
Offer rate			
○ 2 men and a truck - ○ 3 men and a truck -			
Approximate date			
Requested date requested			
NOTES;			
Customer's Email to send company's moving guide			

Movers Guide Checklist Summary

Customer Name	
Customer Email	
Customer Address	
Phone Number	
Projected Move Date	
Estimated Hours/ Weight	
Special Instructions/ Additional Notes	
Completion Date	
Call Back /Survey Sent	

Retail Mover's Guide Checklist

Greet Customer Good Morning, Happy holiday	Record Customers Name
Ask for EMAIL	Current Address

	Is the Move within city?	○ Local Move	○ Out of Town	
	Originating Location	○ Business	○ House	○ Apartment
	Destination	○ Residence	○ Storage Unit	
	Ask how many rooms	○ 2 Bdrm.	○ 3 Bdrm.	○ 4 Bdrm.
	Is there an Upstairs?	○ Yes	○ No	
	Exterior sheds or Guest House?			
	Special types of furniture? ○ Self-adjusting bed ○ fire safe ○ Piano REMARKS ○ Spinet ○ Baby Grand ○ Upright			
	Types of Appliances ○ Refrigerator ○ Washer/Dryer ○ Freezer,			
	Does the customer need packing supplies? ○ Yes ○ No 1.5 Box Wardrobe 3.0 Box Dishpack 4.5 Box TV Box Tape			
	Does the customer need additional Insurance? ○ Yes ○ No			

	Offer rate
	
	  ○ 2 men and a truck -
	  ○ 3 men and a truck -			

	Approximate date			
	Requested date requested			
	NOTES;			
	Customer's Email to send company's moving guide			

Movers Guide Checklist Summary

Customer Name	
Customer Email	
Customer Address	
Phone Number	
Projected Move Date	
Estimated Hours/ Weight	
Special Instructions/ Additional Notes	
Completion Date	
Call Back /Survey Sent	

Thanks to you all for buying my book.

If you like this journal please rate it a 4 or 5 with Amazon. If you are not satisfied feel free to email me at amroybal23@gmail .com